THUG LIFE

A LUST FOR DESTRUCTION

By
CHARLES LOVJOY

MUSCLE GANG PUBLICATIONS

In Association with

TIC MADE ENTERTAINMENT

First Edition

ISBN: 978-1-7359864-0-1

Book cover Artwork concept
By
Charles Lovjoy

Book Cover Artwork Design
By
www.fiverr.com/mithun_02

Audio Book Production and Narration
By
Charles Lovjoy

Other Works

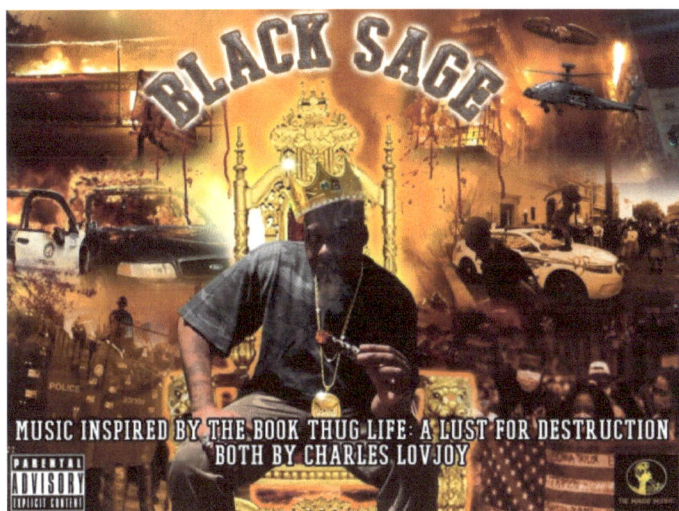

MUSIC INSPIRED BY THE BOOK THUG LIFE: A LUST FOR DESTRUCTION
BOTH BY CHARLES LOVJOY

www.charleslovjoy.com/discography

TABLE OF CONTENTS

TABLE OF CONTENTS

x

DEDICATION

This book is dedicated to all the misguided souls of the earthly realm. Also, the people that society has thrown away and forgotten about, this one's for you!

To Kimyana Reece, thanks for urging, encouraging, and pushing me to finish this authentic piece of literature. You're the best.

Prologue

———— ❧❦❧ ————

A Lust for Destruction:

Whether or not we choose to activate it or not, deep inside every human being is a lust for destruction! Whether it's self-destruction or the destruction of others. It seems like most of us love everything that can potentially kill us! Drugs: cigarettes, alcohol, unprotected sex, junk food.

I mean you name it, we love it! Maybe we're all just programmed to be fucked up! I mean even specific cells inside of our bodies called **T CELLS** only exist to destroy and kill off weaker cells and re-create healthier cells.

Now I know that last line may have been a bit too scientific for a few people, but thankfully this book is not dealing with cell regeneration or scientific destruction. For the sake of this book, I will only be discussing the destruction of society by violence, sex, and murder and how it affects and effects us all individually as well as collectively.

INTRODUCTION

Some say that when you destroy or kill another person, you're actually slowly killing yourself, because the theory is that every living thing on planet earth shares the same energy whether positive or negative. So what is inside of us that causes this lust for destruction? I really want to believe deep down in my heart that no human being actually wants violence and murder on their doorstep in real life.

We don't want it to effect us directly, but for some reason we just can't get enough! We love it! We love the drama, the blood, the guts, and the gore of it all! For some reason society has become numb to violence!

My name is Charles Lovjoy. I am a professional actor, musician, and voice over talent From Detroit Michigan who happens to love marijuana; junk food, Hip Hop, Gangster Rap, Rock & Roll, and scary movies. As an actor and musician,

I've worked with people from all walks of life who share similar interests and experiences. I have gotten the chance to meet and converse with a very interesting array of folks. I'm talking foreign; domestic, filthy rich rich, homeless, poverty stricken, young people, elderly and everyone in between.

Even though I can't say that each encounter was pleasant, I've learned to cherish each personal encounter that I have experienced and will experience in the future. I cherish these encounters not only because it widens my range as an actor, but these encounters also help me vision other people's perspectives from all angles of life. The main thing that I've learned from all of these encounters is that we all share one common bond, the need to love and be loved.

THUG LIFE

A LUST FOR DESTRUCTION

Chapter 1

BIG BUSINESS

These days violence, sex, and murder are everywhere you turn! From video games: to cartoons, to your favorite television programs. Violence, sex, and murder are the daily trending topic on the news! As a matter of fact, the majority of the news seems to be bad news filled with gory true horror stories, yet we the people can't seem to get enough! We actually pay our hard earned dollars to go to the local movie theater and watch violence, sex, and murder on the big screen! We pay cable TV and other streaming subscriptions to feed us violence, sex, and murder on a silver platter!

THUG LIFE

A LUST FOR DESTRUCTION

Even my mother who I consider to be one of the most peaceful human beings on earth, her favorite channel to watch is the ID channel. The ID channel is an ad-supported cable television network that only shows terrible real life horror stories. In every show on the network, someone is getting raped; tortured, kidnapped, or murdered in a horrific manner. Sometimes all of the above!

According to Google and Nielsen data, in 2018 the ID channel was ranked the number one ad-supported cable network for female viewers ages 25-54. The corporation who owns the ID channel isn't the only one profiting from violence, sex, and murder. You see violence, sex, and murder is big business in America. In fact, billions of dollars raked in from violent video games, box offices sales and streaming revenue from violent media is enough to wipe out world poverty FOREVER with still enough left over to see

MILLIONS in profit!

THUG LIFE

A LUST FOR DESTRUCTION

Chapter 2

THE QUESTION IS WHY

Why are humans so obsessed with violence, sex, and murder? Is it genetically installed in us from the moment of conception? Did we inherit it from our ancestors through our DNA? Or is something that is learned? Many people blame it on Hollywood and the media. Some people blame it on rap and rock & roll music. However, like I stated earlier violence, sex, and murder is big business and anyone who knows about business knows that all business revolves around supply and demand. With that being said, if we the people stopped demanding violence; sex, and murder, would there still be a need to supply it?

THUG LIFE

A LUST FOR DESTRUCTION

I love rap music and rock & roll. I also enjoy an occasional horror flick or action movie, but I've always wondered how can some people inflict such violence, destruction and pain on others in real life while others simply view it as entertainment? Whether fiction or non fiction, why do we even chose to view someone else's pain, hurt, and struggle as entertainment? I mean seriously, what the fuck is wrong with us?

Name any time period within any civilization and you will be able to research the cold hard facts that the masses are and always were addicted to and entertained by violence! If you think I'm over exaggerating, just research biblical times when large groups of people would gather to watch public executions such as castrations, beheadings, and crucifixions. Look back at the middle ages when witch hunts took place and many in those communities would gather to watch so called witches receive the death penalty.

—

THUG LIFE

A LUST FOR DESTRUCTION

Think about slavery and how many so called Christian white folks would gather and actually cheer at the public lynching's of African Americans! I don't even know why we call it civilization cause NONE OF THAT SHIT SEEMS CIVILIZED TO ME!

Why do humans seem to have a lust for destruction? Where did it come from, and how do we get rid of it? The truth is that I may never find the answers to most of these questions. However, I do have an answer for the one question referring to people who actually inflict pain; violence, and destruction on others. Well actually, I have a little more than just an answer.

I've actually expounded a theory: hypothesis, and philosophy about the whole shit! When I say the whole shit, I do mean the whole shit! Despite the blame placed on Hollywood: the music industry, and the media for society's lust for destruction, we must take a more in-depth look.

—

THUG LIFE

A LUST FOR DESTRUCTION

THUG LIFE

Chapter 3

DIAGNOSES THUG LIFE

Now before I give you my answer, I must first break down the theory: hypothesis, and philosophy, and where I got it from. In the year 1993 a rapper by the name of Tupac Shakur formed a rap group called Thug Life and even had the words Thug Life tatted on his stomach. Most people thought Thug Life was just a rap group, but for Tupac, T.H.U.G L.I.F.E was actually an acronym for a deep philosophy standing for "The Hate U Give Little Infants Fucks Everyone."

THUG LIFE

A LUST FOR DESTRUCTION

In an interview with MTV, Tupac would later state that "he did not create T.H.U.G L.I.F.E, but only diagnosed it." Back when the late great Tupac first made this self-proclaimed diagnoses of the human condition, I really didn't fully comprehend it or understand the depths of it. But now as a grown man living in this society, I think I finally get it. Tupac actually diagnosed a worldwide multigenerational, multicultural pandemic!

T.H.U.G L.I.F.E! The Hate U Give Little Infants Fucks Everyone. Wow! Could this actually be the reason for so much violence in America and elsewhere? And if the hate u give little infants fucks everyone or T.H.U.G L.I.F.E for short is the diagnoses, then what would be the cure? Now on one hand, some people would not believe where I found the answer and how simple it actually sounds. On the other hand, there will be quite a few people that do believe and understand exactly what I'm talking about!

—

THUG LIFE

A LUST FOR DESTRUCTION

Even though I do not consider myself a Christian, I concur with what the bible says about love. According to the Holy Bible Matthew 22:35-40, the greatest commandment of all is Love. It took me several decades to even comprehend and appreciate why Love is the greatest commandment of all! Through multiple studies and countless hours spent watching documentaries about the world's most hardened criminals, I've come to the realization and conclusion that a lack of love was not only a common bond shared by thugs: rapists, gangsters, bullies, and serial killers, but the lack of love is also often the root cause of their Lust for Destruction.

The majority of murderers: rapists, and other violent criminals often grow up in house holds where there was no real love given, shown, or taught! You rarely hear a case where a serial killer grew up surrounded by love. In fact, the majority of violent criminals often grow up around extremely severe cases of violence; domestic violence, sexual and/or verbal abuse, etc.

—

THUG LIFE

A LUST FOR DESTRUCTION

When I think about Tupac's acronym for T.H.U.G
L.I.F.E "The hate u give little infants fucks everyone,"
Charles Manson, **Aileen Wuornos**, and **Ted Bundy** are just a few
notable serial killers that come to mind!

THUG LIFE

A LUST FOR DESTRUCTION

Chapter 4

MEET THE KILLERS

1. Aileen Wuornos

When the names Charles Manson, Aileen Wuornos, and Ted Bundy are mentioned, most people tend to cringe and only think of the carnage that was left behind. Some people say and think that they all got what they deserved, which was ultimately jail and death. Many only see the violence and pain caused by serial killers without even considering or caring about what actually caused these people to go down a road of extreme violence and lust for destruction.

THUG LIFE

A LUST FOR DESTRUCTION

I do not want to come across like I'm condoning or making excuses for the violent crimes that these people have committed because every individual is responsible for their own actions. However, specific facts should not be ignored. For example, Aileen Wuornos was abandoned by her alcoholic parents at the age of 4 and adopted by her grandparents. Wuornos was repeatedly beaten and sexually abused by her grandfather and one of his friends at a very young age. As a victim of rape, Aileen became pregnant at the tender age of 12 or13! After being put on the streets at the age of 15, Aileen became a prostitute in order to provide herself with money and food.

Aileen eventually went on to be convicted for the murders of 7 men and sentenced to death by lethal injection. Wuornos was executed on the 9th of October in 2002. Yes, Aileen Wuornos did murder 7 people however, since the age of 4 years old Aileen grew up in a household where she was never taught, given, or shown any love! One can't help but wonder would those 7 murder victims still be alive today if Aileen Wuornos had a better childhood?

—

THUG LIFE

A LUST FOR DESTRUCTION

And how different would Aileen Wuornos's life had been if she would've just received love as a child?

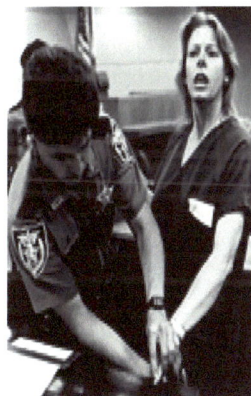

Thug Life

A LUST FOR DESTRUCTION

2. Ted Bundy

Theodore Robert Cowell better known as Ted Bundy is infamously known for kidnapping, rapping, and murdering several women in the 1970's. From the beginning, Bundy's childhood started off entirely on the wrong foot! It is believed that Samuel Cowell (Bundy's maternal grandfather) was actually also his paternal father!

By Ted Bundy's maternal grandfather being his paternal father as well, this also means that his mother is actually his sister too! Basically, Ted Bundy was conceived out of drunken incest: lust, rape, and child abuse. Now if that is not a recipe for destruction and disaster, I don't know what is!

Bundy's own family members often referred to Ted as the spawn of satan because of his grandfather's/father's notorious reputation for racism: fits of rage, verbal, mental, and physical abuse within the household. The most influential person in Ted Bundy's life was his father/grandfather who just so happened to be a violent womanizer: a racist, a child abuser, and a pedophile!

—

THUG LIFE

A LUST FOR DESTRUCTION

Remember the hate u give little infants fucks everyone. Bundy eventually went on to be convicted of several murders: rapes, aggravated kidnappings, burglaries, and attempted murder. He was sentenced to death by electric chair and was executed on January 24th, 1989. It is said that during and after his execution many onlookers sang and danced in celebration of Bundy's death!

4

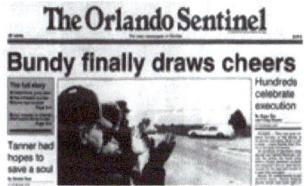

The Orlando Sentinel

Bundy finally draws cheers

5

6

THUG LIFE

A LUST FOR DESTRUCTION

3. Charles Manson

Next, let's take a look into the early life of what perhaps may be the most iconic serial killer of all times, Charles Manson, who's original birth name was Charles Miles Maddox. First of all, Charles Manson never knew his biological father and his mother was a stone-cold alcoholic. Manson's mother Kathleen Maddox was sentenced to 5 years for a robbery when Manson was only 5 years old. Charles would go on to spend all of his teenage years in and out of several foster homes, schools for boys, and other facilities for delinquent juveniles.

In 1947 at the age of 13 while in the Gibault School for boys in Terre Haute Indiana, Charles Manson was reportedly beaten by Catholic priests and suffered strict severe punishments for the slightest acts of insubordination. Charles ran away from that school and a few others that they tried to send him to.

THUG LIFE

A LUST FOR DESTRUCTION

While on the run Manson had no money for survival, so he began a crime spree that involved everything from stealing cars to robbing grocery stores, gas stations, and casinos. Manson was eventually caught and charged with previous crimes. In 1949 age 15, Charles Manson was sent to a reform school called the Indiana Boys School .

While in this school, Charles was often beaten and raped by staff members and other inmates. Charles Manson's criminal record is way too long for me to discuss at this moment, but the bottom line is that Charles Manson's whole life was filled with pain; anger, neglect, violence, and all of his teenage years were spent running from the law.

The Hate U Give Little Infants Fucks Everyone! Charles Manson would ultimately go on to form a cult known as the Manson family and later become one of if not the world's most famous/iconic serial killers.

—

THUG LIFE

A LUST FOR DESTRUCTION

Mr. Charles Manson was initially sentenced to death for the murders of nine people, but his sentence was later reduced to life with the possibility of parole after the state of California abolished the death penalty in 1972. Charles served his life sentence at California State Prison and died while in prison at 83 years old, from a heart attack in 2017.

THUG LIFE

A LUST FOR DESTRUCTION

7

8

9

THUG LIFE

A LUST FOR DESTRUCTION

Thug Life

A LUST FOR DESTRUCTION

Chapter 5

THE APPLE DOESN'T FALL FAR FROM THE TREE

Early on in this book, I asked if the lust for destruction was inherited through DNA. I also asked if it was taught. Oddly enough, I would have to say the answer to both of these questions is yes! Whether directly or indirectly, each generation teaches the upcoming generation how to hate, kill and destroy. For example, if you take your children to see public hangings of several African Americans and they witness you and your friends cheering and having a grand old time, it should be common sense that nine times out of ten those children will grow up to believe there's nothing wrong

---

THUG LIFE

A LUST FOR DESTRUCTION

with hanging African Americans! Those children will in turn teach and breed that same lust for destruction and hatred into their children, so forth and so on. Hate to sound cliché but the old saying is the apple doesn't fall far from the tree.

There are a few exceptions to this famous cliché. For example, there are some people who's childhood was so bad that they're absolutely determined to be better parents than their parents were. Please Don't get me wrong I'm not blaming every parent for every single violent act that was ever committed, but for the most part if you are a gang banger or a racist, your children will more than likely follow in your footsteps because you are the first teacher that your child comes in contact with. The first words a child usually speaks come from words that they hear inside of their households on a regular basis.

Besides parents being a child's first teacher, a child develops his or her entire aura from those who they are around the most. In most cases that just so happens to be the parent or parents.

THUG LIFE

A LUST FOR DESTRUCTION

According to an article from the US National Library of Medicine, "The family provides emotional support to an individual and also plays a significant role in the formation of one's personality." The same article goes on to say, "The quality and nature of the parental nurturance that the child receives will profoundly influence their future development."

Basically, everything that a child is exposed to at the early stages of life becomes a part of their DNA. For example, according to an article in PMC, "Social information alters gene readout in the brain to influence behavior; and genetic variation influences brain function and social behavior." The article also goes on to state that "Brain development, brain activity and behavior depend on both inherited and environmental influences, and variation in behavior shapes the evolution of genomic elements that influence social behavior through the feedback of natural selection."

—

THUG LIFE

A LUST FOR DESTRUCTION

Yeah, that pretty much sounds like a fancy way of saying the apple doesn't fall from the tree. Or better yet, an even fancier way of saying THUG LIFE! We've just been passing down a lust for destruction from generation to generation.

—

THUG LIFE

A LUST FOR DESTRUCTION

Chapter 6

BULLIES SPAWN KILLERS

Even if you are a child or teenager who thinks that it's cool to be a bully, you never know what kind of situation the person you're bullying is facing at home. You never know how close that person is to snapping, blacking out, and killing everybody in sight! Me being from the streets of Detroit Michigan, believe me when I tell you that no one I mean no one is just going to sit there and allow themselves to get bullied too long! Every human being ever created has a breaking point. I believe the proper term is "Fight or Flight."

THUG LIFE

A LUST FOR DESTRUCTION

When a person snaps, sometimes the fight can be about more than one issue. Sometimes you just catch them at the wrong time in their life when they're just fed up with everything! And also, the flight doesn't necessarily mean running for safety. In fact, choosing flight could sometimes mean running from problems and internalizing daily life in a negative way.

This can lead to suicide, homicide, and even mass shootings. In recent studies of mass school shootings, in most cases the shooter either grew up around violence, felt rejected in some manner, was a victim of bullying, or just did not feel loved! Same exact thing with teen suicide. The emergence of social media has actually made it easier for bullies and racists to spread messages of hate to large amounts of people even faster.

I was a child once and I know both sides of the coin. I've been the one bullied and I later became a bully because of it. I know how it feels to get picked on and laughed at by what seems like the entire school. I also know how it feels to

THUG LIFE

A LUST FOR DESTRUCTION

be the one everybody is scared of. The older and wiser I grow, I've come to resent both of those feelings. I feel incredibly fortunate that the universe has allowed me to learn and grow from my ignorance. Words cannot even explain how thankful I am for having certain people in my life that have shown me so many examples of love. I am grateful that I've had several people in my life who's good morals have rubbed off on me.

As a child, sometimes you really can't imagine life for you and your peers as adults. Those that are bullies may never know the deep seed of hatred; insecurity, and/or lust for destruction they have planted inside another. I've actually been fortunate enough to run into a few people that I used to bully as a child. I say fortunate because I was able to humble myself and apologize as an adult for all the mean things I did to them as a child. Unfortunately, a lot of children may never get that chance because mass shootings and other violent acts among children are occurring more frequently these days.

THUG LIFE

A LUST FOR DESTRUCTION

Thug Life

A LUST FOR DESTRUCTION

Chapter 7

———✦———

MESSAGE TO EVERY HOOD; MAKE IT MAKE SENSE

As so-called minorities in the ghettos across America, the system is set up for our demise. Racist cops: judges, prosecutors, and other people in positions of power will stop at nothing to exercise their lust for destruction! As the late great Tupac Shakur once said, "We got whites killing blacks, cops killing blacks, and blacks killing blacks." It completely breaks my spirit to hear about young inner-city African-Americans in places like Chicago, St. Louis, Los Angeles, Detroit, and elsewhere killing each other at such an alarming rate over the simplest of reasons.

—

THUG LIFE

A LUST FOR DESTRUCTION

We already have so many things against us; why be against each other too? When will enough be enough?

Growing up in Detroit, Michigan, I have seen and experienced my fair share of senseless violence. As far as gang culture, I really want to know how a human being can actually hate someone else's guts simply because they're from a different neighborhood? It makes no sense to me what-so-ever, especially when young people have no say-so where their parents decide to live. People are actually killing and dying over neighborhoods where they own no property, have no investments, and never even chose to live there. Just make it make sense!

To all the young gangsters from every hood, you don't understand the power and influence you really have. The same energy/power that you use to take lives could be used to save lives! Even though it is possible to be both, there is a major difference between a gangster and a killer. Killers have no code of honor or ethics, no respect, and no morals. Real gangsters, on the other hand, are usually businessmen

—

THUG LIFE

A LUST FOR DESTRUCTION

who take care of their community, live by a certain moral code, and only kill as a last resort because they know murder is bad for business on so many levels. As a matter of fact, true gangsters often do business deals with gangsters from other neighborhoods because it expands the business's reach.

Real gangsters understand that it's hard to stack money when you have to spend so much to fight murder cases, not to mention the extra heat that murder brings from the feds.

I am from "THE HOOD," and I am also apart of Hip-Hop culture, so I don't want to come off like a hypocrite or like a preacher. With that being said, I understand what it means to be proud and represent where you're from, but I will never understand hating and killing someone else for doing the same thing. Make it make sense!

THUG LIFE

A LUST FOR DESTRUCTION

We are living in an age where cameras are recording our every move. Crooked cops are slaughtering young black people at will and not even serving one day in jail. The tragedy of it all is that in THE HOOD, it seems that we hate each other more than any racist cop or judge ever will! The lust for destruction in the hood is overwhelming.

JUST MAKE IT MAKE SENSE!!

THUG LIFE

A LUST FOR DESTRUCTION

Chapter 2

IT'S UP TO US

    In all actuality, the hate u give little infants really does fuck everyone. Hate and love both are things that are given: received, learned, taught, and possibly inherited. So please be careful and mindful of what you expose the children of the world to, because you actually could be directly or indirectly contributing to fueling the lust for destruction of the next generation of bullies: mass shooters, rapists, pedophiles, and serial killers!

THUG LIFE

A LUST FOR DESTRUCTION

Check on your children! Check on the children in your neighborhood! Make sure these children are not getting abused. After all, the old saying goes "It takes a village to raise a child." You never know, you could be the only glimmer of hope and love in a child's life that could potentially turn their entire life, situation, and circumstances around!

I'm not saying the world will change overnight, but just think of the domino effect a simple thing like love would cause! Think of how many lives that could be effected and affected simply by loving one child and making sure they are not being severely abused. Think about all of the teens that probably wouldn't have committed suicide if they were not being bullied online or in school! Imagine if you could have prevented a mass shooting. Imagine if you could have been the one person in Charles Manson's life who prevented him from becoming a cult leader and serial killer!

—

THUG LIFE

A LUST FOR DESTRUCTION

In closing, it really does not make any sense to me that we've come so far and have all this knowledge and new-age technology yet violence: rape, murder, and hate crimes are at an all-time high in today's society! T.H.UG. L.I.F.E. is the diagnoses, but LOVE is the vaccine!

We must get back to loving each other or we'll all be fucked! We have to realize that only loving our own children, family, and friends is just half of the battle, because that one child down the street from you who nobody bothered to love could be the one that shoots up your child's school!

The gospel of Matthew 12:25 in the Bible says "Every kingdom divided against it's self is brought to desolation: and every house divided against itself shall not stand." Well, the Earth is that kingdom! We humans are that house! In my opinion, Love should be under the same umbrella as water: sunshine, and oxygen. Meaning we all need it to live and grow because life without love just ain't life. It is not natural, and it is also not how human life was intended   to   be.

—

THUG LIFE

A LUST FOR DESTRUCTION

Please just remember THUG LIFE. The Hate U Give Little Infants Fucks Everyone! Everything ugly in the world: violence, pain, neglect, racism, sexism, and fear was taught and spread to us as infants.

WE THE PEOPLE MUST BREAK THE VICIOUS CYCLE OF HATE!! We have to stop blaming everything else because

I'TS UP TO US AND ONLY US!!

THUG LIFE

A LUST FOR DESTRUCTION

ACKNOWLEDGEMENTS

This literary work was inspired by my observation of the human condition in the 20th century. It is based on facts and my opinion of those facts! Special thanks to those who have taught and/or shown me love in any shape form or fashion. The people that inspire me every day! Shabazz Ford; Jerry Ford, Kenneth Morris Jr., Terry Collins, Kimyana Reece. Thank you to all my cousins for inspiring me to want to make a better future for the youth.

To my cousin Latoya Simpson Smith, thank you for being my big sister and showing me the perfect example of what I should look for in a woman; intelligence, loyalty, and ambition. I want to thank my aunt Gilda Simpson Gause for teaching me how to cook because I loves me some food! (Laughing   out   loud)

THUG LIFE

A LUST FOR DESTRUCTION

Thank you to my uncle Kelvin Simpson for being the father figure that was missing from my life! Thank you to my cousin Rhonda English for helping me to choose acting over street life. Thank you to my cousin John Lampkin Jr. for driving me and my mom to court all those times I fucked up as a juvenile.

Thank you to my creator for designing my brain and my heart. And last but definitely not least, I want to thank my mother Darnell Simpson and my grandmother Alberta Simpson for choosing to love me and teaching me how to love!

—

THUG LIFE

A LUST FOR DESTRUCTION

In Loving Memory of:

Alberta Simpson

Daunte Morgan

Kelvin Jerome Simpson

Kelvin Simpson III

Michael Steele

Christopher Cobb

Jaun Raybon

THUG LIFE

A LUST FOR DESTRUCTION

For those that support my work, I really appreciate you.

Thank you.

THUG LIFE

A LUST FOR DESTRUCTION

ABOUT AUTHOR

Charles Lovjoy

Though I have been blessed with many talents, my first love/passion has always been writing! My most recent projects include a non-fiction book titled "Thug Life: A Lust for Destruction," and the accompanying music for the book, a hip-hop album entitled "Black Sage."

THUG LIFE

A LUST FOR DESTRUCTION

Whether music, songs, screenplays, fiction or non-fiction, writing to me is extremely therapeutic. **Through my works, I intend to provoke thoughtful insights on the human condition and how we view it.**

My name is Charles Lovjoy. I hail from Detroit, Michigan. From a young age, I nurtured a deep love for the entertainment industry, which has dictated much of my life's course. By the age of nine, I was writing songs, short stories, and poetry. Since 2011, I have been acting and doing voice-overs. You can call me a "Jack of All Trades." I'm a professional actor, hip-hop artist, producer, writer, author, and voice-over talent.

As a rap artist, I have shared a stage with some very notable hip hop acts, such as; Scarface, Twista, D-12, Bone Thugs-N-Harmony, Too short, and many others. Some of my most notable projects to date include; voice-overs for The Detroit Pistons and Detroit Tigers and a guest appearance on The Comedy Central Network on a show called "Detroiters."

—

THUG LIFE

A LUST FOR DESTRUCTION

Being a staunch believer in continuous learning and self-improvement, I have a rich educational background that accentuates my career as an artist. I pursued a degree in Audio Communications from the prestigious Specs Howard School of Broadcast Arts and studied Music Production at Full Sail University. In high school and college, I took up several acting classes to hone my acting skills and knowledge. Throughout my career, I've been fortunate enough to interact with people from all walks of life, making me compassionate and respectful towards other cultures.

For more information visit www.charleslovjoy.com

THUG LIFE

A LUST FOR DESTRUCTION

THUG LIFE

A LUST FOR DESTRUCTION

WORK CITED

The Path of a Serial Killer." *Professor Ramos' Blog*, 13 Dec. 2019, professorramos.blog/2019/12/13/aileen-wuornos-the-path-of-a-serial-killer/.

Jjfletcherbooks, ~. "True Crime: Aileen Wuornos." *JJ Fletcher Books*, 14 Mar. 2019, jjfletcherbooks.com/2019/03/14/true-crime-aileen-wuornos/.

"Aileen Wuornos." *Biography.com*, A&E Networks Television, 10 Sept. 2019, www.biography.com/crime-figure/aileen-wuornos.

"NSFW: A Look Back At Ted Bundy's Execution." *True Crime Magazine*, 20 May 2020, **www.thecrimemag.com/nsfw-a-look-back-at-ted-bundys-execution/**.

THUG LIFE

A LUST FOR DESTRUCTION

Weiner, Jeff. "Ted Bundy Was Executed 30 Years Ago Today. Serial Killer's Fate Was Sealed in Orlando." *Orlandosentinel.com*, Orlando Sentinel, 24 Jan. 2019, **www.orlandosentinel.com/news/breaking-news/os-ne-ted-bundy-orlando-executed-30-years-20190123-story.html**. (newspapapers.com)

Photos of Ted Bundy: (From left to right) Bettmann/Contributor/Getty Images & Universal History Archive/Contributor/Getty Images & Bettmann/Contributor/Getty Images & Bride Lane Library/Popperfoto/Getty Images Janos, Adam. "How Ted Bundy Was Able to Change His Appearance So Easily." *A&E*, 21 Feb. 2019, **www.aetv.com/real-crime/ted-bundys-many-faces-serial-killer-change-appearance-eyes**.

"Young Charles Manson and His Mother Kathleen Maddox: Charles Manson, Manson, Charles." *Pinterest*, **www.pinterest.com/pin/773000723517423715/**. (charlesmanson.com)

THUG LIFE

A LUST FOR DESTRUCTION

"Pin on Nostalgia Pictures / Hollywood '2.'" *Pinterest*, **www.pinterest.com/pin/187180928238693492/**. (time.com)

"What Happened to the Manson 'Family'? A Look at Key Figures, Decades after Horrific Murders." *Los Angeles Times*, Los Angeles Times, 30 July 2019, **www.latimes.com/california/story/2019-07-30/where-are-they-now-charles-mansons-family-decades-after-horrific-murders**.

"What Happened to the Manson 'Family'? A Look at Key Figures, Decades after Horrific Murders." *Los Angeles Times*, Los Angeles Times, 30 July 2019, **www.latimes.com/california/story/2019-07-30/where-are-they-now-charles-mansons-family-decades-after-horrific-murders**.

Study of family factors in association with behavior problems amongst children of 6-18 years age group. Jogdand SS, Naik J. Int J Appl Basic Med Res. 2014

THUG LIFE

A LUST FOR DESTRUCTION

Jul;4(2):86-9. doi: 10.4103/2229-516X.136783. PMID: 25143882 **Genes and social behavior.**

Robinson GE, Fernald RD, Clayton DF. Science. 2008 Nov 7;322(5903):896-900. doi: 10.1126/science.1159277. PMID: 18988841

First Edition

ISBN: 978-1-7359864-0-1

Book cover Artwork concept
By
Charles Lovjoy

Book Cover Artwork Design
By
www.fiverr.com/mithun_02

Audio Book Production and Narration
By
Charles Lovjoy